A
HIGHER PURPOSE

Living a Life of Meaning and Significance

Jim Reger

ISBN: 978-1-4669-0567-2 (sc)
ISBN: 978-1-4669-0565-8 (hc)
ISBN: 978-1-4669-0566-5 (e)

Library of Congress Control Number: 2011961347

Trafford rev. 01/17/2012

 www.trafford.com

North America & International
toll-free: 1 888 232 4444 (USA & Canada)
phone: 250 383 6864 ♦ fax: 812 355 4082

CONTENTS

PROLOGUE

It started as a feeling—someone or something was trying to wake me up from the inside. I felt distressed and confused and fewer things made sense—but I couldn't explain why or what was happening. I now know that awakening starts with confusion which leads to an awareness that there is an absence of meaning and purpose in our lives. We feel lost. We are not clear about what's important. These are the signs that we are on a spiritual search:

- Why am I here?
- What am I supposed to be doing?
- How do I articulate the meaning and purpose of my life?
- Who am I—beyond my positions and possessions and my achievements?
- What matters the most to me?
- What are my deepest, unfulfilled dreams, passions, and gifts?
- What kind of a contribution am I making to the world—beyond my own self-interest?
- What is the point of my life?

We don't easily deal with these questions about ourselves because we know, at some deep level, that the answers will require us to change.

When we can acknowledge, to ourselves, that our lives don't make complete sense—we are at a potentially crucial point. This acknowledgement is often the beginning place for finding new meaning and significance and a higher purpose for living.

From the time I can remember thinking as a child, I have somehow always believed there had to be a reason for our existence. What were all the struggles about? Was it just a random sequence of events? Were the people who came in and out of my life there strictly by chance? I started to question the significance of life early on, but I think many people don't explore the deeper meaning of life because they fear there may not be one. But I chose to believe, at a very basic level, that our purpose is to evolve—to learn and to grow—and that the search for meaning is the central human experience.

I spent much of my life around people who worried about money and the stuff it can buy. How do we make more of it? How do we get more stuff? How do we get fancier stuff? And when they aren't thinking about getting more, they are concerned about who has more than they do? And why? And do they deserve it?

What a great way to spend our time and energy. We must eventually realize that none of it matters. We can't take it with us. But if money doesn't matter—what does? What are the things we can take with us? Struggling to genuinely answer this question is living a life of higher purpose.

This book is a collection of thoughts about finding meaning and purpose in our lives. Most of the thoughts are mine, but I have included some inspiring quotes from other individuals as well. These thoughts and quotes are loosely organized into seven chapters, but they can be read in almost any order; and, as none of them are longer than a few sentences, you can spend a few seconds or a few minutes reading and then put the book down. The entire book can be read in an hour or two.

My wish is that you find some inspiration to continue your own individual journey towards finding *meaning and significance in your life*.

DEDICATION

This book is dedicated to my loving father, Frank Reger

Acknowledgments

This book is a result of the assistance from an amazing and diverse group of individuals who participated in my growth and supported me in innumerable ways.

To Joan, my wife and best friend for over forty years—thank you for providing the love, strength, forgiveness, and support necessary for me to have the courage to explore my authentic self. Thank you for assisting me to be who I am. I cannot think of a greater gift.

To Natasha, my warm-hearted daughter, who changed my life forever the day she was born—thank you for the love I feel from you every day.

To Brayden, my son, who is the most authentic person I know—thank you for our conversations about life and its mysteries and magic. You are a wise old soul, and I am grateful for your presence in my life.

To all those who contributed in so many ways to this book:

- David Irvine
- Casey Norberg
- Tim Andrew
- Ryan Pettersen
- Bruce Dyck
- Leslie Dickinson
- George DeLure
- Brad Potentier
- Greg Baynton
- Bob Tewsley
- Jordy Harris

- Nancy Cooper
- Steve Young
- Lorne Schnell
- Kim Dalton
- Dave Brown
- Laurie Peck
- Walt Nicholson
- Brian Rodgers
- Brett Large
- Marie Sturman
- Oliver Jervis

INTRODUCTION

This is a book about thoughts. I've always been intrigued by thoughts and the power they have in our lives. And now, in my late sixties, having had a successful entrepreneurial career, having watched my kids grow into adults, and having celebrated over forty years of marriage; it is abundantly clear to me that my life is living proof that the emotional intensity and amount of time that I applied to a thought had a direct relationship to what results showed up in my life—financially, in relationships, or by any other measure.

Because I enjoy thoughts, I have always enjoyed reading. In my case, I was more interested in books that challenged me to evolve my thinking and appealed to my curiosity. I was never much for reading strictly for entertainment value. When my wife and I would go off on those "reading" holidays, she would consume mystery novels; and I would consume books on philosophy, psychology, and spirituality. She was somehow naturally spiritually evolved—I had to work at it.

I also always enjoyed books of quotes—because they were usually short, straight-forward thoughts that got me thinking in a new direction—opening up new perspectives and challenging my current views about things. I read quotes from all sorts of folks—from famous ones to those who had no claim to fame whatsoever. While I was busy creating and growing a fast-track career in the information technology industry, while simultaneously raising a young family, I had precious little time to read books that were meant to be read from start to finish, with a beginning, a middle, and an end. So, I became attracted more to books of quotes and books that I referred to as "books of thoughts;" because I could pick up the book, read it for five minutes or fifty minutes, and get value—even if I knew I wouldn't have time to pick the book up again for weeks or even months. Often, just reading a sentence or a paragraph would challenge my current state of mind and create a new perspective on an issue that I was contemplating. At other times, I would discover a notion that I'd been wrestling with would be reinforced or stated in a way that brought clarity to my thinking.

One of my favorite books, which I have read many times over the past thirty-five years, is such a book. It is a book on life, on living, on loving, and on our relationships—with others and with oneself. I can pick it up, read it for as long as I wish and put it down. Each time, different thoughts have different meanings for me. Even though I made my living from an industry that changed rapidly, my experience from life revealed that people do not really change all that much. We are still inspired by the same needs (the need to belong), and face the same fears (fear of rejection) and similar issues that we faced hundreds of years ago.

My life has been a search for meaning and significance. The *thoughts* and *quotes* in this book have provided me with the greatest inspiration for reflection. I hope you take this book home—pick it up, put it down, reflect—and pick it up again and again.

Jim Reger

CHAPTER ONE

The Awakening

"When faced with our own immortality, we no longer have time for insignificant matters—we have a greater calling beyond mere survival and the gratification of materialistic things that we have been conditioned to acquire. Our perspective changes and we recognize that we have a higher purpose in life. We do have a spiritual nature, a spiritual origin, and a spiritual destiny. What a shame it would be not to respond to our spiritual voice. When we listen, we will learn or remember who we really are."

Jim

"If you are unaware and deny that there is any level of higher wisdom and guidance to your life, then the guidance must come through the density of physical events. Awareness first enters into an unaware personality through crisis.

. . . The awakening of the personality to the potential of the soul has come to require the loss of a mate, or the death of a child, or the collapse of a business, or some situation that renders the individual powerless. It requires the failure of external power.

. . . No understanding of evolution is adequate that does not have at its core that we are on a journey toward authentic power, and that authentic empowerment is the goal of our evolutionary process and the purpose of our being. We are evolving from a species that pursues external power into a species that pursues authentic power."

Gary Zukav
The Seat of the Soul

"*Those on the journey to living a higher-purpose life have a tenacious desire to live a life of meaning and significance.* They tend to seek deeper, more loving and compassionate relationships. They live in the present and with a greater awareness of what they wish to create in their lives. They set their own moral standards, and one of their dominant qualities is a great respect for all of life. They recognize that the past is behind them, the future is the state towards which they are growing and the present is the path that will get them there. *Their craft is the art of living, and they are their own work of art.*"

Jim

"The spiritual quest usually begins as a search for purpose and meaning."

Jim

"As we negotiate the curves and corners of our lives, we must continually give up parts of ourselves. The pain of giving up is the pain of death, but death of the old is birth of the new."

M. Scott Peck, M.D.
The Road Less Travelled

"What do you want beyond economic and materialistic success? *You often are clear about what you don't want before you are clear about what you do want.* This question can be frustrating until you realize that you have to stop in order to change direction. The more certain you are about what you don't want, the sooner you will gain clarity about what is truly important. Be prepared to learn that there can be a difference between what you thought you wanted and what you really want. If you are uncertain about what you want and what is really important, you are bound to feel incomplete. This is a spiritual crisis; it is your soul's way of telling you to 'wake up.' If you recognize that the cause of the crisis is within, then you may become receptive to guidance that you would not have welcomed before; and then real change can begin, even though you fear what you may hear."

Jim

"All men should learn before they die, what they are running from, and to, and why".

James Thurber

"People can accept the inescapable fact of mortality. What frightens them more is the dread of insignificance, the notion that we will be born and live and one day die and none of it will matter . . . . people understand that the story of their lives has to have a beginning, a middle, and an end. But what they desperately want is to live long enough to get it right, to feel that they have done something worthwhile with their lives, however long."

Harold S. Kushner
Living a Life that Matters

"We are all here to evolve at some level. We can evolve consciously or unconsciously, but we will evolve. Wouldn't it be better to evolve on purpose?"

Jim

"When we enter a period of meaningful change in our lives, it is reassuring to know that there are many others on the same journey—and that there are roadmaps."

Jim

"Any authentic search for our purpose and meaning must lead within. While it is normal to begin this search somewhere else, enlightenment is an inside job."

Jim

"A search for meaning and significance often begins when we can let go of being measured by what we have, rather than who we are."

Jim

"To leave the world a bit better, whether by a healthy child, a garden patch, or a redeemed social condition; to know that even one life has breathed easier because you lived—that is to have succeeded."

Ralph Waldo Emerson

"When I visit my hometown, where I grew up as a kid, and run into my former neighbors, teachers and coaches; I always use Mr. or Mrs. when speaking to them. Yet, at my age, and while I do respect them; there is no need for me to use these titles, but I do because of this respect. I somehow feel this need because I still want to feel someone is in charge—just like I did when I was young. Did you ever wonder who is in charge of keeping it all in order, ensuring that it would eventually all make sense? I spent many years believing that politicians or religious leaders were supposed to be in charge and would straighten things out when things went astray. But my innocence died a long time ago, and I asked myself 'If they aren't in charge, who is?' Is it possible that no one is in charge? Just me?"

Jim

CHAPTER TWO

Purpose

"Choose your thoughts carefully,
They will make your life.

Stay curious and open to learning,
As this is the key to growth.

Have laughter as a part of each day,
It is music from your soul.

Always give others your best,
This is the road to success.

Forgive all who wish you ill,
It is a gift to yourself,

And live with gratitude, humility, compassion and love.
For this is your higher purpose."

Jim

"Our higher purpose in life is to become who we are—our authentic, spiritual self."

Jim

"Spiritually evolved people, by virtue of their discipline, mastery and love, are people of extraordinary competence, and in their competence they are called on to serve the world, and in their love they answer the call. They are inevitably, therefore, people of great power, although the world may generally behold them as quite ordinary people, since more often than not they will exercise their power in quiet or even hidden ways."

M. Scott Peck, M.D.
The Road Less Traveled

"Those who choose to live a higher-purpose life are generally not encouraged by the masses."

Jim

"Everybody is dealt a hand in life; most people are afraid to play their hand or get mired in resentments over not receiving better cards. Wouldn't it be better to play it out as best we can, even with insufficient advice and information along the way?"

Bennet Wong & Jock McKeen
The New Manual for Life

"Our higher purpose is where we have our greatest passion. When we are living a life of higher purpose, we are living a life of passion."

Jim

"It seems the more I learn, the more questions arise; and I am learning that's how it's supposed to be. Our purpose in living is to learn what we need to learn and to assist others to do the same. We are all learning and teaching. We are leading and following at the same time, giving and receiving—and the more we give, the more we receive. How we perceive others is generally rooted in how we perceive ourselves."

Jim

"Success without happiness is the worst kind of failure."

Author Unknown

"When we assume that we are already enlightened, spiritual evolution has stopped."

Jim

"To find yourself demands that you have the courage to reject society's definitions of success and create your own."

Jim

"If enlightenment can be described as the knowledge of ourselves, we can say that becoming enlightened is a work in progress."

Jim

"Life is our classroom, and we are all students and teachers."

Jim

"The best way to prepare yourself for life-changing decisions is to make everyday decisions with your higher purpose in mind."

Jim

"We all have a mission here on earth—a higher purpose to serve; and if you are still alive, it isn't finished."

Jim

"We teach others primarily through how we live our lives. Your life then becomes your greatest imprint on the world."

Jim

"When we walk to the edge of all the light we have and take the first step into the darkness of the unknown we must believe one of two things will happen—there will be something solid for us to stand on—or we will be taught to fly."

Claire Morris
Source Unknown

"Even though society ridicules those who follow their inner voice and serve their higher purpose, history often claims them as its legendary heroes."

Jim

"The purpose of life is a life of purpose."

Robert Byrne

"Evolution is a process of continuous transformation."

Bennet Wong & Jock McKeen
The New Manual for Life

"There is a spectacle grander than the sky, and it is the interior of the soul."

Victor Hugo

"What each of us seeks is the fulfillment of our own potential."

David Irvine
Simple Living in a Complex World

"Man's search for meaning is a primary force in his life."

Victor Frankl

"Spirituality, unlike religion, is an individual experience; and seeking our higher purpose can initially be frightening. But what if the only purpose in life was to be content and happy? Why would we fear this?"

Jim

"When you find yourself feeling uncertain, remember that you have a higher purpose. By choosing to go higher, you rise above your doubts and set-backs."

Jim

"You either have to take the initiative to go to the places with your life that you want to go to—or it will never happen. Where do you want to go with your life? What is holding you back and what are you waiting for—an invitation?"

Jim

CHAPTER THREE

Cultural Influences

"The cultures that we are exposed to, especially early in life, play a significant role in determining our beliefs and significantly influence the results we create in our lives. Each culture has a shared belief system, about the world and ways of dealing with it—how things are and how they should be. It is very powerful to be in a 'family' of people with shared opinions, values, principles and traditions. We eventually learn how shattering it can be when we are excluded from these cultural groups; and if we question them, we are often excluded. Cultures seldom encourage their members to question them, but we must do just this if we are to seriously evolve spiritually. Evaluating our prejudices, opinions, values and beliefs and discarding those that no longer fit our conscious assessment of who we are is a necessity for personal growth. These spiritual 'crossroads' are opportunities for seeking a higher purpose in our lives. Ultimately, it is we alone who must become our own greatest teacher. If not ourselves, who should we choose to write our own story of our future?"

Jim

"From your thought springs your reality. From your ideas your future emerges. Thus, your beliefs create your behaviors, and your behaviors create your experience. What you believe, therefore, becomes a most important thing."

Neale Donald Walsch
Tomorrow's God—our Greatest Spiritual Challenge

"Examine your beliefs—If you would be a real seeker after truth, it is necessary that, at least once in your life you doubt, as far as possible, all things."

Rene Descartes

"Spiritual evolution is a process of constant death and rebirth. Old beliefs die and new ones are born. This is the process of personal transformation, which is a constant fact of life; and the moment we wholeheartedly embrace it, life takes on greater significance. We then can see our higher purpose as an on-going process of self-discovery and renewal."

Jim

"Your cultures create your beliefs.
  Your beliefs create your attitudes.
    Your attitudes create your judgments.
      Your judgments create your behavior.
        Your behavior creates your results."

Jim

"The journey to authentic power requires that you become conscious of all that you feel. "

Gary Zukav
The Seat of the Soul

"The more we study and learn about beliefs from other cultures, the more we understand that our perceptions about life are based upon very narrow and limiting views of the universe."

Jim

"There is no value-judgment more important to man—no factor more decisive in his psychological development and motivation—than the estimate he passes on himself."

Nathaniel Branden

"When we choose to believe in someone, or something, we give that belief tremendous power in our lives. It pays to be very conscious of to whom, and to what, you give power and authority in your life."

Jim

"Your 'truth' about anything is merely your individual perception of truth. If you accept that your truth is the only possible correct one, you limit your understanding and potential to evolve. Being fixed in any belief is a barrier to self-insight."

Jim

"The lessons we have to learn will be presented to us over and over until we learn them. In my own life, the consequences of not learning have always been more severe each time I have to repeat the lesson."

Jim

"The voice of authenticity is a whisper from within. If you wish to hear that whisper you must turn off the noise of culture and create an environment, a sanctuary, a place where you can attune to that still small voice."

David Irvine
Becoming Real: Journey to Authenticity

"I have yet to meet a person who worships money who will acknowledge that they have enough. Scarcity thinking seems to be part of their beliefs. No matter how much they have, someone else will always have more. By comparing themselves to those who have more, they sabotage their self-worth."

Jim

"If that 'higher self' within us is to be born, or better, revealed, it is our cultural self that must, in effect, die."

Joseph Chilton Pearce
The Biology of Transcendence—A Blueprint of the Human Spirit

"We are 'supposed' to know who we are—I mean this is one of the basic questions in life, and yet at times it seems like the most difficult question there is. When we don't know who we are, or what our purpose is, or if we find ourselves describing ourselves by our 'positions' and 'roles', new fears arise. We lose our sense of identity and our connection to our treasured cultures."

Jim

"We do not believe the world we see. We see the world we believe."

Jim

CHAPTER FOUR

Becoming Ourselves

"Everyone has more than one singular, 'self.' When we talk about our 'self,' it helps to be aware that we usually have three different 'self's';

- The cultures by which we have been influenced have created a 'model self' for us to compare to for acceptance in those cultures;
- We have our spiritual 'authentic self', which is who we have always been; and,
- Somewhere in between, we construct a 'self-image'—which reflects our own current view of 'the kind of person we are'.

Much of our life is spent trying to reconcile the difference between what the culture is telling us we 'should' be doing and what our true authentic self knows is right for us. The wider the gap, the greater the internal conflict and turmoil we will experience.

Seeking approval from the cultural 'model self' is an external focus, whereas seeking approval from our 'authentic self' is an internal focus. Genuine meaning and significance comes as we focus our attention away from the external world towards the internal world. *When we see ourselves as our greatest resource, we are living a life of higher purpose.*"

Jim

"Anxiety is often caused by the guilt of not living up to the 'model self' defined by an external culture. But it is also caused by a sense of meaninglessness. The best way to overcome anxiety is to seek self-knowledge. When you choose to not follow the 'model self,' you become a threat and can risk going through a painful process. This is often the price you pay for developing a mind of your own."

Jim

"Being true to your 'authentic self' is the only way to develop spiritual integrity, and it is not an easy path. *It takes courage to be you*. When we compromise who we are, our 'authentic self,' to gain the acceptance or approval of others, we give up a piece of our soul. We are our most powerful 'self' when we do not need external approval."

Jim

"Many high achievers become independent, and seem very free and powerful; yet, in their attachment to the approval and attention of others, they remain tied and limited. They are independent, but not free."

Bennet Wong & Jock McKeen
The New Manual for Life

"One of the most difficult lessons we, as adults, must learn is to recapture the sense of honesty which was so keen and powerful in childhood. Young children who are not even aware that honesty is a virtue have such a keen sense of speaking directly, truthfully, and openly that even when they are taught to be kind, tactful, and polite, their sense of honesty remains so spontaneous that they persist in saying what they feel no matter how severe the consequences may be. Only after repeated correction, disapproval, punishment, and rejection does the child submit and learn the gains of distortion, subtlety, and deviation. Only then does the social need for kindness and sympathy, for achievement and reward, for success and approval, exceed the determination to remain true to one's own eyes and ears and heart. When we are not honest, we are cut off from a significant resource of ourselves, a vital dimension that is necessary for unity and wholeness. A significant stream of inner life is dammed up, and until we can recapture and recreate that sense of honesty we cannot know ourselves and we cannot know other persons and grow as individuals and in relationships."

Clark E. Moustakas
Finding Yourself, Finding Others

"For those who aspire to become more authentic, more real and more spiritual, there is no better school than life. Daily living offers so much potential for growth and development because of the demands it places on us. Your life, with all the people you love and dislike, is your best classroom. If you can see that life is one giant learning and teaching opportunity, you will evolve much more effectively by paying attention to life. However, you must pay attention!!"

Jim

"It hurts to be defeated by conscience, to feel compelled to take the more demanding high road, to resist temptation, to apologize. But I suspect it hurts more to keep winning out over conscience. Too often, we compromise our integrity; we do something we really don't believe in doing, to reach some important goal, only to find one of two frustrating things happening: Either we gain the prize and realize it wasn't worth gaining, or we end up with neither the prize nor our integrity."

Harold S. Kushner
Living a Life that Matters

"The greater your uncertainty—the greater the potential lesson."

Jim

"Far too often we allow ourselves to talk about the wrong things in life. So many of us are silent about what matters most, the deepest part of ourselves. We talk about cars and sports, hair, appearances, and clothes as we remain silent about our dreams, our hopes, and our values. We are mute about our deepest concerns, passions, and fears."

David Irvine
Simple Living in a Complex World

"The only thing that keeps us from becoming all that we are capable of becoming is our unwillingness to look within."

Jim

"Of all the forms of fear—fear of being misunderstood, of being diminished, of becoming vulnerable—none is more thwarting than the fear of rejection. For most people partial communication and relationship are preferred to the risks of honesty and openness of self-expression and self-disclosure."

Clark E. Moustakas
Finding Yourself, Finding Others

"Seeking approval from yourself instead of others is a deeply spiritual experience."

Jim

"The only conquest necessary in life is to win over ourselves."

Jim

"When we can see through ourselves, we don't need to worry about whether anyone else will."

Jim

"When you have control over yourself, there is no need to have control over others."

Jim

"There is nothing to be rid of, or added to, or punished for; there is only more self-awareness and self-responsibility to be experienced. There is no need to struggle toward perfection; each person is already whole. Instead of striving, people can devote themselves to know and to accept themselves in the process of self-compassion."

Bennet Wong & Jock McKeen
The New Manual for Life

"If you understand yourself more in the evening than you did in the morning, it has been a great day."

Jim

"The best way to get over feeling sorry for yourself is to appreciate yourself."

Dan Baker, Ph.D.
What Happy People Know

"To become who we are, we often have to get out of our own way."

Jim

CHAPTER FIVE

Change and Transformation

"There is no such thing as 'too late' in life. We are always free to change our minds—and, therefore, our lives."

Jim

"If you accept that you have free will and the power to choose, then you must know that changing your life is always a possibility."

Jim

"Transformation is the ever-unfolding expression of deep knowledge of the self. The more thoroughly people know their patterns and tendencies, the more varied, creative, and spontaneous they can be. What others claim to be 'change', we identify as transformation. In transforming, nothing new has been added. Individuals can only become more fully alive, more aware, more creative and more in touch with their place in relationship to others and to the universe as a whole. In short, all that they can become is more of themselves."

Bennet Wong & Jock McKeen
The New Manual for Life

"The fear of change is so powerful in many people that it prevents them from even attempting to make a positive change."

Jim

"We can never really change another person. We can manipulate them or threaten them and cause a short-term difference in their behavior, but the only true way to effect a change in our relationship with them is to change ourselves. *The only true way to change the world around you is to change the world within you.*"

Jim

"Being vulnerable is a sign that we are evolving. Vulnerability reduces stress and anxiety enabling us to deal effectively with change."

Jim

"Many people won't change until it is literally forced upon them, often by a serious event like the death of a loved one or illness. We sense some kind of security in things staying the same, even if we aren't happy with the way they are. Yet, if we don't grow, we stagnate. To grow means we must submit to a temporary loss of security. And, the more secure we are with who we are, the easier and less frightening change becomes."

Jim

"People handle their fear of change in different ways, but the fear is inescapable if they are in fact to change. Courage is not the absence of fear; it is the making of action in spite of fear, the moving out against the resistance engendered by fear into the unknown and into the future. On some level spiritual growth, and therefore love, always requires courage and involves risk."

M. Scott Peck, M.D.
The Road Less Travelled

"In order to feel comfortable with personal change, we need to focus on our higher purpose—which is to expand our self-awareness, pay attention to what, and who, is in our lives, and make choices."

Jim

"Every time we deal with change, we will pass through fear and discomfort and evolve our soul towards our higher purpose."

Jim

"When I was young and free and my imagination had no limits, I dreamed of changing the world; as I grew older and wiser I discovered the world would not change, so I shortened my sights somewhat and decided to change my country, but it too seemed immovable. As I grew into my twilight years, in one last desperate attempt, I settled for changing only my family, those closest to me. But alas, they would have none of it! And now I realize as I lie on my deathbed, if I had only changed myself first, then, by example, I might have changed my family. From their aspirations and encouragement I would have then been able to better my country, and who knows, I might have even changed the world."

Inscribed at the tomb of an Anglican Bishop in Westminster Abbey
David Irvine
Simple Living in a Complex World

"One of the best ways to change our lives is through service to a higher purpose—assisting others through acts of kindness and compassion."

Jim

"When you are seeking a life of meaning and significance, be aware that boredom is a sign that you should bring about change in your life, as you are not learning from the present situation. The best antidote to boredom is to learn something about yourself."

Jim

"One positive change would be to start understanding ourselves instead of criticizing or apologizing for ourselves."

Jim

"First you must change yourself. Then—and only then—can you change your world."

Neale Donald Walsch
Tomorrow's God—our Greatest Spiritual Challenge

"If you are currently living the life you want—congratulations—you are in the minority. If you aren't—you will likely have to give up the life you have in order to get the one you want. By definition, this implies you will have to change."

Jim

"The journey of transforming ourselves has no end."

Jim

"There is really only one alternative to personal transformation—and that is denial."

Jim

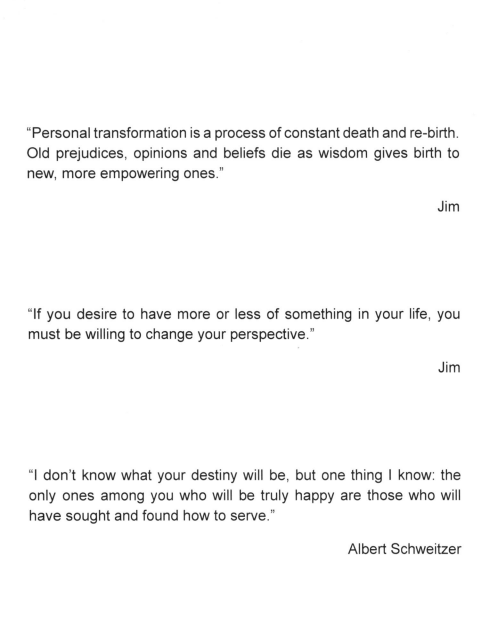

"Personal transformation is a process of constant death and re-birth. Old prejudices, opinions and beliefs die as wisdom gives birth to new, more empowering ones."

Jim

"If you desire to have more or less of something in your life, you must be willing to change your perspective."

Jim

"I don't know what your destiny will be, but one thing I know: the only ones among you who will be truly happy are those who will have sought and found how to serve."

Albert Schweitzer

"I am amazed at humankind's incredible contradiction—always wanting change in our lives without working for it. We want more love, money and happiness. We want less stress and conflict—as long as it doesn't mean we have to change ourselves. How badly must we want our lives to be different before we will change?"

Jim

"Change takes but an instant. It is the resistance to change that can take a lifetime."

Hebrew Proverb

"All effective personal transformations and evolutions begin with a willingness to change or with a personal crisis. Which do you think is less painful?"

Jim

"Instead of feeling guilty about your mistakes, search and find the lesson. *Mistakes are gifts on the path to growth*."

Jim

Chapter Six

Choice

"Deciding that you will be the author of your own story is a huge step towards living a life with a higher purpose."

Jim

"One of the greatest gifts we are given is the gift of *free will*—the power to choose who we will become and what we will do with our lives. We become more authentic and in alignment with our higher purpose in life, choice by choice. By consciously choosing to forgive, to be more compassionate, more loving and understanding of ourselves; we become more forgiving, compassionate, loving and understanding of others."

Jim

"Choice is always available, but it takes courage to exercise it fully. Choice is the foundation of hope. It is only when we feel that we have no choices that fear sets in. You always have choices."

Jim

"I've learned that every morning when I get up I can choose to either feel good or feel bad for that day. I decide, 'Oh, what the hell' and I decide to feel good. That's how I've lived so long."

Age102—Unknown Source

"Uncertainty means you are questioning and stepping back from quick judgments. With patience and tolerance for uncertainty, a new form of certainty will evolve."

Jim

"Man arises as a unique person through the medium of choice. A good choice is one that is derived authentically: on the basis of self-awareness and self-determined inquiry and action, the person develops the ability to make free and autonomous decisions. The freedom to make choices and to learn from them is the core of being and the basis of all individuality."

Clark E. Moustakas
Finding Yourself, Finding Others

"Somewhere today, at this moment, a girl is choosing to be a ballerina, a boy is choosing to be an actor, a young couple is choosing to raise a family. These choices will have a major effect on their future. What decisions could you be making today, at this moment, which could have a major effect on your future?"

Jim

"Every choice we make has consequences; and, therefore, our lives are ultimately a reflection of the choices we make. If you make everyday choices with your higher purpose clearly in mind, you will become more committed to your authentic presence, and your consequences will reflect your choices."

Jim

"When most people forgive they do not want those that they forgave to forget that they forgave and forgot. This is not forgiveness. It is a means of acquiring external power over another."

Gary Zukav
The Seat of the Soul

"Changing your mind about what you want from life can be very positive. But if you do this from a place of 'giving up' on your authentic dreams, it can be a terrible shock to your soul."

Jim

"Try choosing forgiveness over anger or resentment. Ask anyone who has truly forgiven another, and you'll likely hear how freeing this choice is. Who do you need to forgive—if not for their sake, for yours? Forgiveness isn't about forgetting. Forgiveness is about letting go of your anger, hurt, or hate and rising to a higher purpose. When you let go of your resentments, you gain a wealth of self-love."

Jim

"Take responsibility for the choices you make in your life and be respectful of the choices that other's make in theirs. They aren't 'wrong'—they are merely different choices that they need to make for their own growth."

Jim

"Many will one day wake up and realize that not everything we envisioned doing, or becoming, in our lives is going to become reality. Some of them just won't happen. But while many reach this place in despair, you can choose to seize the opportunity to go higher. Sift through these things and eliminate those that are taking your attention away from focusing on what is truly important."

Jim

"Man alone is the architect of his destiny. The greatest revolution is that human beings, by changing the inner attitudes of their minds, can change the outer aspects of their lives."

William James

"When faced with a difficult choice, try this before choosing. Look at the situation from the point of view of your cultural 'model self' and consider the consequences of a choice in that direction. Then do the same from the perspective of your spiritual 'authentic self'. Only after you have considered both perspectives, and the corresponding consequences, should you make a choice. This is choosing consciously in the present, and you will be more content with choices made this way."

Jim

"You are always a student in life. If you are alive, you are learning. However, what you learn is your choice. *Learn on purpose.*"

Jim

"Avoid putting yourself before others, and you can become a leader among men."

Lao-Tse

"Our greatest gift is free will—our ability to select our own thoughts and to make our own choices—minute by minute."

Jim

"Those who are truly committed to the transformative process of becoming who they are (their authentic spiritual self), pay attention to the present. The choices made in the present are the transformative ones. Choose wisely. Choose with clarity—the clarity that you have a higher purpose and that is the place to live from. Choose always love over fear, and you will wisely choose to have humility, gratitude, forgiveness, and compassion in your heart. Choose to be accountable and responsible for your own experiences, and respectful of the experiences that others have chosen. Choose with courageous action when faced with fear."

Jim

"Whenever we seek to avoid the responsibility for our own behavior, we do so by attempting to give that responsibility to some other individual or organization or entity. But this means we then give away our power to that entity, be it 'fate' or 'society' or the government or the corporation or our boss.

We have the freedom to choose every step of the way the manner in which we are going to respond to and deal with these forces."

M. Scott Peck, M.D.
The Road Less Travelled

"If you could chuck it all—the appointment book, the cell phone, the e-mails, the in-box, the 'toys'—and start over, who would you be? You have a choice about how to spend the rest of your life. Choose to evolve."

Jim

"*Failure is one of life's greatest teachers*. The lesson is about what you take from the failure and apply in your life. So, in a strange and curious way, failing is really winning."

Jim

"Our world reflects the basic thought form that there is no afterlife, that in this lifetime the only thing that insures power is what can be had and gained. Sometimes we speak of an afterlife, but we do not really believe that after we leave the Earth we are still responsible for the choices that we have made upon the Earth or our choices would be very different."

Gary Zukav
The Seat of the Soul

"Whenever you don't know *what to do*, just do *what's right*—irrespective of the consequences."

Jim

"There is a story about a Native American tribal leader describing his own inner struggles. He said, 'There are two dogs inside me. One of the dogs is mean and evil. The other dog is good. The mean dog fights the good dog all the time.' Someone asked him which dog usually wins, and after a moment's reflection, he answered, 'The one I feed the most'."

Harold S. Kushner
Living a Life that Matters

"You have attracted to you everything that is in your life. What you do with it is your choice."

Jim

"Rather than focusing our attention on what we do not want, a higher choice is found in identifying that which we choose to bring into our lives, and living from that perspective."

Gregg Braden
The Isaiah Effect—Decoding the
Lost Science of Prayer and Prophecy

"You will be the happiest when you are in the company of those whose concept of happiness is the same as your own."

Jim

"Good people will do good things, lots of them, because they are good people. They will do bad things because they are human. In the daily, if not hourly, wrestling matches that set the tone of our lives, sometimes the angel wins and sometimes the angel loses. With luck, we will not be overwhelmed by guilt when the egotistical impulse defeats the angel, and we will understand that the victory is temporary, not permanent, when the angel wins. We will understand that, to be human, we need them both. But we will never stop asking ourselves, what kind of person do I want to be?"

Harold S. Kushner
Living a Life that Matters

"A mature person is one who is willing to change his or her mind—it is a sign of learning."

Jim

"All of us will be victims of cruelty, thoughtless behavior, and petty annoyances. At times like that, we will have to choose between the seductive appeal of getting even, attractive but harmful to our souls, and the cleansing force of integrity, reclaiming power over our lives precisely by not giving in to the temptation to get even. And we will know which side the angel is on . . ."

Harold S. Kushner
Living a Life that Matters

"If you wish to become a different person, make daily choices towards that direction."

Jim

CHAPTER SEVEN

Love, Fear and Happiness

"There are many ambitious people who are terribly unhappy, because they equate their self-worth with their net-worth. Ambition is a much admired quality in western society, yet it is often a result of revenge for some frustration from our past—unloving parents, rejections from teachers, other social groups, or some other type of emotional deprivation as a child. Unfortunately, when we are driven by a need to succeed, we will sacrifice our family, our health, our friends and, most importantly, our own happiness. We need to be clear that our lives have a purpose beyond the acquisition of 'stuff'. By focusing more on self-expression, love, learning, and on making a contribution, we will find our higher purpose and be happier."

Jim

"Those who truly love themselves seldom experience anger, as most anger is a response to feelings of being unworthy or of having been victimized in some way. When we feel victimized or unworthy, we tend to blame ourselves or someone else for those feelings. Blame is a call to *anger*—giving away control of our feelings to someone else. All blame is a waste of time. No one benefits when we blame."

Jim

"Happiness is a state of being within people, for which they are fully responsible. Because of this, individuals can choose to be happy over anything, including money. Unfortunately, most people don't have the opportunity of creating happiness over money; so all they can do is fantasize about it. Those with money can easily squander it on things and activities of little consequence, resulting in little enjoyment. Some people create happiness for themselves wherever they go, in whatever they do; the money only increases the style and variety of things with which they will do that."

Bennet Wong & Jock McKeen
The New Manual for Life

"The principal form that the work of love takes is attention. When we love another we give him or her our attention; we attend to that person's growth. When we love ourselves, we attend to our own growth."

M. Scott Peck, M.D.
The Road Less Traveled

"Feel not what your mind tells you, but what your heart tells you."

Gary Zukav
The Seat of the Soul

"Feeling victimized is one of fear's faces. We feel victimized because we fear the future, or we are resentful and grieving over the past. We create communities of victims which, in turn, have created a huge industry of therapists, psychologists, psychiatrists, and lawyers who are the benefactors of serving these communities. Only you can victimize yourself, and those who choose the victim role are seldom happy people. If you truly want happiness, you must realize that it is not a gift provided to us by someone else, or something only lucky people are entitled to. Genuine happiness is a sense of knowing your true, authentic self. It is an inner satisfaction. It is achieved by recognizing that you have a much higher purpose. *If we can't find happiness within ourselves, we won't find it anywhere else.*"

Jim

"The work we do in our lives is our love made visible."

Kahlil Gibran

"Acquiring knowledge is the best way to overcome a fear."

Jim

"Listen to your child enough and you will come to realize that he or she is quite an extraordinary individual. And the more extraordinary you realize your child to be, the more you will be willing to listen. And the more you will learn."

M. Scott Peck, M.D.
The Road Less Traveled

"When negative thoughts come into your mind, you can be curious and observe them and inspire yourself with the knowledge that you have a higher purpose."

Jim

"To reach the light on the other side of your fears requires that you courageously walk through the darkness to get there."

Jim

"The more children know that you value them, that you consider them extraordinary people, the more willing they will be to listen to you and afford you the same esteem."

M. Scott Peck, M.D.
The Road Less Traveled

"It is tempting to believe that before you can love another, you must first learn how to love yourself; but it is more likely that you will learn to love yourself while you learn to love another. By bringing yourself forward and revealing yourself to another (an act of intimacy), you will discover how distant from others you have been, and how split off from yourself you have become."

Bennet Wong & Jock McKeen
The New Manual for Life

"It takes very little to be happy, and the fastest way to create happiness for yourself is to create happiness for another."

Neale Donald Walsch
Tomorrow's God—our Greatest Spiritual Challenge

"True listening is love in action."

M. Scott Peck, M.D.
The Road Less Traveled

"Behind fear is the opportunity to love and grow."

Tim Andrew

"When I genuinely love I am extending myself, and when I am extending myself I am growing. The more I love, the longer I love, the larger I become. Genuine love is self-replenishing. The more I nurture the spiritual growth of others, the more my own spiritual growth is nurtured. I am a totally selfish human being. I never do something for somebody else but that I do it for myself."

M. Scott Peck, M.D.
The Road Less Traveled

"Happy people get their status from within. Their status symbols are things like a happy family, good friends, and pride in their work."

Dan Baker, Ph.D.
What Happy People Know

"It is impossible to be in a state of love and a state of fear at the same time as they are mutually exclusive; and, therefore, the best antidote to fear is love."

Jim

"Many of the wisest spiritual leaders believe the only thing that ultimately matters at the end of your life is the quality of your love."

Jim

About the Author

Jim Reger's passion for and commitment to facilitating powerful and effective change within individuals and organizations is evident in his work, which is focused on assisting leaders in creating and building authentic lives and cultures for themselves, their organizations, their families, and their communities. Thousands of business owners and executives have attended Jim's thought-provoking and inspiring presentations on leadership, purposeful living, and creating shared visions. Jim is founder of The Reger Group (www.regergroup.com), a family business specializing in delivering intensive entrepreneurial development programs. Jim and his daughter, Natasha, work extensively with business families, addressing the special challenges they face as they move through the life cycles and struggle with the unique effects that family dynamics have on their businesses and their lives.

Jim is also the cofounder of the Newport Institute for Authentic Living (www.newportinstitute.com), and he has authored the following books:

- *Future Work: The Ultimate Guide to the Employment Possibilities of the Future*
- *The Authentic Leader: It's About PRESENCE, Not Position* (co-authored with David Irvine, best-selling author of five books)
- *Bridges of Trust: Making Accountability Authentic* (also co-authored with David Irvine)

My Personal Story

For as long as I can remember, I have been passionate about discovering life's deeper meaning and purpose.

My father's tragic suicide when I was seven years old forced my mother to work more than full-time to support her three young children, and I was left pretty much on my own to figure out my place in the universe.

Thinking back, it is obvious that I made two key decisions at that time. The first decision was that I would never again withstand the pain of having a cherished loved one taken away from me. The strategy I subconsciously employed to accomplish this was to build a "brick wall" around myself, thinking that if I never let anyone get close to me I would never again have to feel the kind of pain that comes from losing someone I loved. The second decision was that I would not be poor. The stress of not being able to adequately support his family had been a huge factor in my father's departure. So I, incorrectly, made the assumption that financial security and a happy home life are synonymous.

After my father's death, the next most significant defining moment in my life was the birth of Natasha, my daughter, when I was twenty-eight years old. I can vividly remember questioning myself at the time about what value there could possibly be in having a wall between one's self and one's child—even a wall that was a single brick thick, let alone hundreds! That day my wall came down, and not just a brick at a time—I brought in the bulldozers.

The whole issue of leadership now took on new meaning as it became apparent that the only true meaningful and honest way to demonstrate leadership to my child would be how I led my life—which led me to question everything about myself. "Who am I really?" and "How will I lead my life so that I can demonstrate to my child what I hold as important?" became consuming thoughts. They subsequently led me on a never-ending journey to find my real and authentic self. I read, studied, took courses, and pursued every opportunity I could find to learn and to experience more about who I was and what the events of my life and the people in it were meant to teach me. My old beliefs about needing money to have a happy home life were challenged daily as I struggled to find a balance between the time and energy needed for a successful career and the desire to be with my family.

Four years later, the scales were totally tipped in favor of having quality time with my family when my son, Brayden, was born. Deciding that there would be other opportunities for business ventures, I left a successful career and took my wife and two children to Hawaii. We spent almost a year "hanging out" at the beach. I got to be a kid with my kids during the year before my daughter started school and a new chapter in our lives as a family began. This was a defining year in my life. I realized just how much can be learned from our children. They were instrumental in helping me gain a solid sense of myself and what mattered most in my life. From this solid grounding, I was able to rebalance my life. From a more secure place, I threw myself into new entrepreneurial ventures, taking along a passion for imparting my authentic self and my family values into my leadership style.

The next ten years were the happiest years of my life. We grew as a family, and I grew into a more open person, learning to know and love myself at a deeper lever, and thereby being able to love and connect with other people more fully. While still passionate about my work, it never consumed me again because I had let go of the notion that my worth as a husband, father and individual was in any way connected to my net worth.

These years were filled with meditation and a deep spiritual search to find out more about who I really was and then live my life from this authentic place. It was primarily during this period that I formed a solid basis of meaning in my life and became focused about my true purpose in life, the principles that I would live by, and the choices that would assist me in creating the results I wanted.

Over the past twenty five years, I have worked with thousands of executives and entrepreneurs, with the primary focus of my efforts being to assist them in determining what is most important in their lives, to identify their higher purpose, to find their *authentic* self, and to integrate this knowledge into how they lead and learn in their businesses, communities, and families.